followership

1. the capacity or willingness to follow a leader.
2. a group of followers or supporters: following.

followership

1. the capacity or willingness to follow a leader.
2. a group of followers or supporters: following.

Joshua McElhaney

followership

ISBN: 9781540894922

Printed in the U.S.A. by CoffeeHouse Publisher

ackowledgements

This book's contents were written and taught as a series when I was the Lead Pastor of Life Church in Tyler, TX. The series originated in early 2016 to develop our members into dynamic followers. I want to acknowledge the wonderful congregation of Life Church. Without their unwavering followership, our leadership team would never have been as successful as it was.

dedication

This book is dedicated to the incredible saints of Life Church in Tyler, TX. Thank you for allowing me the privilege of leading you for those short years.

contents

introduction
- leadership

Leadership is the very fiber of what makes America great. From pioneers who ventured out across this land of promise, escaping political oppression and pursuing religious freedom, to great presidents who navigated this nation across the pages of history, effective leadership is at the core of America's success.

Franklin D. Roosevelt, one of our nation's most influential presidents, left behind a premier leadership legacy. Afflicted with polio at the age of 29, which left him paralyzed in both of his legs, Roosevelt never allowed the effects of this disease to bind him with restrictions, however, neither physically nor mentally. Roosevelt's never-say-never attitude was contagious—so much so that he was voted in as president of the United States during one of America's most critical and fearsome decades in the year 1933.

At this time, America was deep in the throes of the Great Depression. Searching for hope, America found it in the most unlikely of heroes. Roosevelt was the only president to be elected to four consecutive terms in our nation's history, and he served as president of the United

States until he died in 1945.

Roosevelt's leadership was on full display as he led the American military into WWII, and his impeccable courage was instrumental in America's rise to power. His political knowledge, intellectual influence, and yearning to persevere are characteristics that every good leader longs to possess.

Our country is blessed with such a rich history of incredible leaders. Many books have been written, many seminars have been held, and many men have been exalted as leadership gurus. Yet, if we are honest, one factor of leadership is often missing—not some magical formula or revolutionary missing link: what I'm talking about is what empowers leaders to lead.

We tend to glamorize leaders such as Franklin D. Roosevelt, and they are undoubtedly due much respect. Where would we be without these great pillars of strength, these concrete examples of leadership? From a young age, many of us aspire to one day make an impact—to influence our generation's lives through leadership.

I've been blessed to work with some incredible young leaders, and I've been privileged to influence their lives. As I survey the future generation of leaders, I believe we are willing to pay the price to be great, and this is certainly something we need in this critical hour.

Unfortunately, the result of our obsession with leadership is that we have created a dangerous paradigm for leaders as they seek the will of God for their lives. Often, in our zeal to be leaders, we bypass a critical stage in our development. In our enthusiasm to influence young minds, in our efforts to equip, train, and empower the younger generation, we have neglected one of the greatest assets to leadership development: followership.

In post-modern culture, we don't tend to glamorize being a follower. After all, who wants to be second? We didn't invest our lives in leadership and ministry to play second fiddle. We want to use our God-given gifts and natural abilities to lead.

However, the truth remains that there's never been a great leader who wasn't first a follower. There has never been an individual who impacted thousands, or even millions of lives, who didn't at one time or another learn the value of following.

This book will delve into a reality of solid leadership: that before you can lead effectively, you must learn to follow. This concept you may have never contemplated will drastically alter your thought process and prepare you for the journey of leadership. It is not leadership in itself, but it is a prerequisite for decisive leadership. It is followership, the flipside of being a leader.

chapter 1
- what is followership?

Followership. If you've never heard the term, you are not alone. It's not that following is a new concept; it's just one that is often readily overlooked or forgotten. Our generation has created a cultural phenomenon concerning the leadership hierarchy. A leader's position is highly esteemed, while we often view those who follow as unimportant or insignificant.

Leadership is an interactive venture: leaders depend on followers and vice versa. Today's world puts a high value on team effort, and effective team effort requires that team members effectively follow.

In many ways, followers set the bar for leadership. By submitting to a leader's authority, the follower validates the leader's influence in his or her own life, in turn, leaving an impression on others.

It is often said that a leader without followers is simply taking a walk alone.

In many ways, it is more critical for leaders to understand followers than for followers to understand leaders. Often, in business and religious settings, we create monarchial systems of leadership. We ignore the servant

It is often said that a leader without followers is simply taking a walk alone.

followership

class, and the leader leads out of a position of power.

This method rarely works efficiently. Followers in these types of environments often resent their leader, and in some cases, they revolt against the power. One cannot demand influence and respect from a perch of power; one must cultivate influence through an atmosphere of service.

If leaders took the time and the effort to get to know their followers, they would see greater efficiency in their churches and businesses. By learning about who you lead and understanding what drives and motivates them, you discover how to tap into their potential.

So, where do we start in coming to understand such a complex subject as followership? As is the case in any topic related to ministry, we should look to Jesus Christ. Many people fail to realize the significance of Jesus' following. We must understand how He set up this unique paradigm of leadership and followership from studying the New Testament.

One significant aspect of Jesus' ministry is that he built it around followers, not leaders. The first command Jesus ever gave on earth was, "Follow me." What a great perspective we gain when we pause long enough to examine the unique nature in which Jesus conducted His ministry.

Before we dive into that aspect of this book, let us first take a more straightforward approach to understand followership fundamentals.

Followership can be defined as "the willingness to cooperate in working toward accomplishing the group mission, demonstrating a high degree of teamwork, and building cohesion among the group." It sounds a lot like leadership.

Effective followership is an excellent building block for effective leadership. Traits, habits, and knowledge gained through following translate well into the role of leadership. In other words, how well you eventually lead may very well depend on how well you currently follow.

When searching for information, there are numerous sources to which one can turn to find helpful tips on effective leadership, on leadership practices, and on how to reach your full potential in leadership.

Unfortunately, there isn't much information available on how to be a great follower. Let's begin by examining followership and the attributes necessary to be a great follower.

Here are a few fundamental characteristics of influential followers:

SERVICE

Influential followers don't need to be asked to do something. They take it upon themselves to do it. For example, if an event happens at church or on the job, an effective follower will make it their mission to be present and be involved.

Too often, we are content being a spectator when we should purpose to be a participator. We can get involved by volunteering to help mow the grass, clean up after events, teach Bible studies, or pick up people for church. If you want to become the best leader you can be, it starts here.

Typically, in our church, we assign responsibilities

based on need. Sometimes we allow our young ministers to preach; sometimes, we rely on them to help in other ways. It may not be as significant to you personally to volunteer your time for a church garage sale, but it is significant to the church. Even when there is no glory to be gained, a willingness to be involved is the first sign of a great follower.

When you're asked to do something that seems menial or insignificant, be willing to do it. Don't let yourself fall prey to the lie that because of your God-given talents or callings, you're above doing unglamorous tasks. If that means taking out smelly trash or cleaning a filthy restroom, do it.

In the book of Acts, the apostles found themselves entrenched in controversy:

> *"And in those days, when the number of disciples was multiplied, there arose a murmuring of the Grecians against the Hebrews, because their widows were neglected in the daily ministration"* (Acts 6:1)

As the church began to grow, a dispute arose among the disciples. One sect of Jews, the Grecians, felt neglected and perceived that special treatment was given to the Hebrew widows while overlooking the Grecian widows.

These widows gave everything to the church, and as a result, became impoverished. They were relying on people when they had a need. There was a daily ministration; they checked on everybody and made sure everyone has everything they need. The problem is this; 12 apostles are watching over 5,000 people.

The Grecians were Greek-speaking people. They grew up outside of Israel. The Hebrews were Jewish natives who had never left. These Grecians would have traveled to Jerusalem for the feast of Pentecost and most likely became converts in Acts 2 when the Holy Ghost's initial outpouring changed everything.

> *"Then the twelve called the multitude of the disciples unto them, and said, It is not reason that we should leave the word of God, and serve tables"* (Acts 6:2)

The Apostles' response does not imply that the twelve disciples felt the serving was beneath them; they had been serving since the beginning. Instead, they understood that they were insufficient to meet the needs of these people. More importantly, in trying to do so, they were burning themselves out. If they were to spread their time and energy to serve the region's widows, they would neglect their priority of preaching of the Word. It is not that they are "too good" to serve tables; serving tables would distract their focus.

Every leader begins by serving; they grow by delegating. So they appointed deacons—"seven men of honest report, full of the Holy Ghost and wisdom." These men became overseers of the business side of ministry.

Look at the list of deacons "servants" appointed: Stephen, Philip, Prochorus, Nicanor, Timon, Parmenas, and Nicolas. These are all Greek names. This reality teaches us two lessons:

First, the Hebrew part of the church did not hold on to any idea of "seniority" or "superiority" but let the most qualified people serve. The most qualified person for the job isn't always the leader.

Secondly, if you can identify a problem or desire something to be done, God wants to use you to fix it! These were Greek deacons; it was the Greeks who recognized the issue, so the apostles appointed them to fix it.

What is the result of the Apostles' sharing ministry?

"And the word of God increased; and the number of the disciples multiplied in Jerusalem greatly; and a great company of the priests were obedient to the faith." (Acts 6:7)

Chapter 6 is a pivotal moment in the book of Acts when the church experiences "growing pains." It is here that the leaders appoint the first seven "deacons" to shoulder some of the responsibility of ministry – because the church cannot grow effectively if we expect those who lead us and preach to us also to handle all the other ministry responsibilities. These seven men are not exceptionally gifted, nor are they politically empowered – in fact, in Greek "diakonos," the word deacon means "a servant."

They did not appoint more leaders so that they would have more people in a position. They set more leaders so that the church would have more servants.

Spiritually immature people in the church have many more needs (and are much more likely to feel "neglected") than established saints. That is not to say that they are necessarily wrong. When church problems come to our attention, it allows us to exercise our faith, faith in the Lord, and faith in our leaders, that they have a solution that will benefit the church and each other. The events here were not a compassion problem as the devil tried to make it out to be; this was a structural problem. The early church was not afraid to adjust its structure to make room for ministry. It took leaders willing to delegate and followers ready to serve. Delegation and serving are the never-ending cycles of influential followers.

I understand that for many of us, serving food to widows doesn't sound like the kind of ministry to which we believe God has called us. Shouldn't someone with less potential oversee these tasks? The answer is no. If you want to develop as a leader, you must first prove yourself a servant.

The prophet Elijah is one of those biblical leaders whose example demands our attention. Whether you are a novice in scripture or a scholar of the Word, you can appreciate the standard of leadership Elijah sets. What I find most incredible about Elijah is not how his story ends, but how it began.

We tend to overlook the vehicle that carried this pioneer to his prominence, and by doing so, we create a vacuum of disappointment in our ministries.

First, God tells Elijah in I Kings 17:2-3 to go and hide. Three years later, God would speak to Elijah again and say, *"Go show yourself."*

For three years, Elijah would attend God's school of ministry. He would be lonely and in need, and he would watch as God supplied.

Before Elijah could show himself in a position of power, he first had to hide in an attitude of obedience. Here's what we must learn from this: if I can't hide my talent and abilities behind someone else, God will never elevate me to show my skills and abilities to the world. Ministry and service are not about me.

Elijah would never forget what he learned in his time of hiding or how that experience impacted his development as a leader. When God called Elijah to place his mantle of leadership over the next generation through Elisha, Elijah helped develop Elisha by asking him to pour water over his hands in service.

Anointed to be a leader, Elisha poured the waters of service before he ever parted Jordan's waters.

There is no such thing as a job that is beneath you. If you desire leadership, service is your ticket.

Acts 6 sets an example of this. It wouldn't be long before Stephen, an early-church deacon appointed by the twelve disciples, would be stoned for his preaching. Amidst the chaos of the hostile crowd stood a zealous young man named Saul of Tarsus. Saul was there to hold the coats of those who were casting stones.

As calloused as his heart may have been at the time, Saul had to have been impacted when he heard Stephen, full of the Holy Ghost, look up steadfastly toward Heaven and proclaim, *"Behold, I see the heavens opened, and the Son of Man standing on the right hand of God"* (Acts 7:55-56)

Stephen was more than a waiter of tables. He was full of the Holy Ghost. He planted a seed that would sprout forth in Acts 9 when Saul met Jesus for himself on Damascus' road. For Stephen, the tables of service were the preparation for ministry.

Philip, another of the deacons chosen in Acts 6, soon also found himself in uncharted waters. In Samaria, a place

There is no such thing as a job that is beneath you. If you desire leadership, service is your ticket.

followership

Jews typically wouldn't dare venture, Philip introduced the revival that broke open the door for Gentile believers. It wasn't one of the twelve who accomplished this but a young man willing to wait tables.

Don't ever discredit opportunities to serve; God orchestrates them all. Keep your spirit humble, stay full of the Holy Ghost, and know that your service can make an impact, too.

LOYALTY

Influential followers will not be participators in negative conversations about their church or their church's leadership team. This principle applies in the business world as well.

Have you ever observed a diehard sports team fan? They're called fans for a reason. A fan is an abbreviation of the word fanatic. Have you ever been around a fan and mistakenly said something negative about his team?

One cold December night, my dad took me to a Dallas Cowboys game. I was in junior high, and this was an incredible thrill for me. I was a huge Dallas Cowboys fan, even though they weren't particularly good at the time.

This night was bitterly cold. The wind swirled through the corridors of that old Texas Stadium. I'm confident that my body was frozen down to the bones that night.

The Cowboys were playing one of their greatest nemeses, the New York "Football" Giants. The Cowboys had the lead all night long until a late touchdown drive by then-quarterback Kerry Collins put the Giants up for good in the final minutes of the fourth quarter.

I'll never forget: A few rows up from us was an obnoxious Giants fan. The Cowboys fans nearby had been letting him have it during the game. So naturally, when his Giants went up, he turned the tables. There was just one problem. We were in Dallas!

A fight soon broke out as an obviously drunk yet very loyal mob attacked the man for his distasteful actions and commentary about their team.

As influential followers, we should be just as loyal to our church and our leadership as are these crazed fanatics who blow hard-earned money to cheer for people they'll never meet. We shouldn't get involved in drunken brawls, but we should be quick to shut down potentially harmful conversations about our church, pastor, or any leader.

Influential followers love their church, their pastor, their leadership, brothers, and sisters and are loyal to them.

AN AGREEABLE SPIRIT

A church is a conglomeration of personalities and backgrounds. We will never agree on methodology one hundred percent of the time.

When I was a Pastor, I encouraged our leaders to voice any concerns regarding my decisions. The leadership team received a vision-casting form at the close of each year. The purpose of the form was to encourage them to voice any disagreements or differing views regarding the church's direction. Some things work, others don't. We don't want to bog down our leaders with programs or processes that simply don't work.

Although we may disagree on a few fundamentals of methodology, an effective follower will always support the Pastor or leader's decision and work with those in leadership to fulfill the vision.

The Bible reveals a beautiful illustration of this principle. In Exodus 25, we are given a detailed description of God's mercy seat and the cherubim that were to reside on each end of the mercy seat.

> *"And the cherubims shall stretch forth their wings on high, covering the mercy seat with their wings, and their faces shall look one to another; toward the mercy seat shall the faces of the cherubims be"* (Exodus 25:20)

As these golden cherubim stretched over the mercy seat, their wings were to touch as their faces pointed toward the mercy seat.

Although unified, these cherubim didn't look eye to eye with one another. Although they may not have seen eye to eye, their wings met in unity.

To be an effective follower, you must look beyond petty disagreements and personal preferences to embrace a spirit of unity with those in authority.

You may not see eye to eye on every church matter or every issue at work, but you have a responsibility to support your leadership's vision. Bind together with your leaders and assist them in the pursuit of their dream.

A POSITIVE ATTITUDE

Life is tough. Trials and circumstances visit us all, and at times, these hardships originate from within the church walls.

As influential followers, we shouldn't allow ourselves to become thermometers that reflect conditions around us. Instead, we should be thermostats that control the temperatures of our attitudes and emotions.

The Bible records an interesting exchange as the Apostle Paul stood before King Agrippa. Agrippa permitted Paul to defend himself against the myriad of complaints that had been laid at his charge. As Paul turned to look Agrippa in the eye, he said, *"I think myself happy, king Agrippa, because I shall answer for myself this day before thee touching all the things whereof I am accused of the Jews"* (Acts 26:2)

I love Paul's response! Facing certain death and false accusations, Paul didn't allow circumstances to determine his attitude.

Most people think that positivity comes from good circumstances. That's not the case at all. It appears Paul knew a secret:

> *"A man hath joy by the answer of his mouth: and a word spoken in due season, how good is it!"* (Proverbs 15:23)

It's not circumstances that should determine your attitude but a commitment to looking for positives in all situations and maintaining a healthy mindset.

Choose your response to circumstances. Don't allow petty issues to turn you into a grouch; respond with positivity! Your response to situations makes them either better or worse.

BEING A TEAM PLAYER

One of the most challenging aspects of followership is that a hundred different people with a hundred different personalities have to learn to achieve a common goal. Their motive can't be recognition or a desire for personal accolades. They must be driven by a desire to see the church thrive.

Sometimes you won't get recognized for things you do, and that's ok. God keeps excellent records! You will be blessed for your faithfulness. Influential followers don't need recognition; they have a purpose.

> *"And we know that all things work together for good to them that love God, to them who are the called according to his purpose"* (Romans 8:28)

When you live for His purpose and not your own, you have a promise that everything will work out for your good. Don't allow selfish ambitions to motivate you; be driven by His purpose.

To build a team concept, we must overcome some challenges. We must reject the idea of ME to embrace the idea of WE.

Steps to building a great team:

- Cut along the dotted line and rotate 180 degrees.
- **ME** must become **WE**.

followership

It can no longer be about what is best for me, but what is best for the team? It can't be about who gets the credit, who's preaching the sermon, or who taught the Bible Study. Did the team win? That's all that matters.

"Some indeed preach Christ from envy and rivalry, but others from good will. The latter do it out of love, knowing that I am put here for the defense of the gospel. The former proclaim Christ out of selfish ambition, not sincerely but thinking to afflict me in my imprisonment. What then? Only that in every way, whether in pretense or in truth, Christ is proclaimed, and in that I rejoice." (Philippians 1:15-18 ESV)

The Apostle Paul was in chains, in a Roman prison. His critics were preaching Christ from envy and rivalry. It was selfish ambition. Interestingly the KJV uses the word contention. It means "to canvass for office, to get people to support you." Paul aimed to glorify Christ and get people to follow Him; his critics aimed to promote themselves and win a following of their own. Instead of asking, *"Have you trusted Christ?"* they asked, *"Whose side are you on—ours or Paul's?"*

He was able to rejoice, not in his critics' selfishness, but in the fact that Christ was being preached. There was no envy in Paul's heart. It mattered not that some were for him, and some were against him. All that mattered was the preaching of the gospel of Jesus Christ.

If Paul were a ME minister, he would've spent his energy in prison discrediting those critical of him. Instead, Paul was a WE minister. Rather than discrediting his critics, Paul rejoiced. He didn't care who preached; as long as the kingdom advanced, Paul rejoiced.

None of us have the same level of critics that Paul did. None of us have people opposing us and trying to threaten our lives just for living for God. If Paul can celebrate the Gospel's advancement with people who wanted him dead, I can celebrate the kingdom's progress with like-minded brothers and sisters.

chapter 2
-the team concept

So, what makes the team great? We've already established that there is no I in team, so we know that it's not great individuals that make up a great team. Many times in sports, the best teams don't even have the best players.

One of the greatest mistakes we've ever made in leadership is thinking that we can do it all independently. That's simply not the case

We often misunderstand teamwork to mean that everyone on the team is equal. That's not the case at all. If you've ever played sports, or even paid attention to sports, you learn quickly that great teams have teammates who know their place.

A great team will have a leader or a captain, it will have specialty players who specialize in one thing, and role players who do the dirty work.

What makes an effective team is when the team members understand who they are and what they add to the team.

The team concept is a Biblical concept. Jesus didn't have a solo ministry; Jesus had a team of 12 disciples. As I said earlier about teams, Jesus was the leader; then you had Peter, James, and John, and then you had the rest. Each guy knew his place within the framework of the team.

How do we build an effective leadership team? It begins in a way you may not expect. It starts with you. To create a leadership team, first God must make the leader.

One of the hardest things to do is to allow God the time to do what he needs to do to prepare us to succeed.

One time I had a young man become very frustrated with me. He was a natural go-getter, and his personality wanted to storm Hell with a water pistol, one of those types. He had grand plans. He approached me a few times wanting to implement his ideas. To everything he brought me, I said no. One day his frustration boiled over, and he called me and asked if we could meet and have a conversation.

In his zeal to see his vision come to fruition, he failed to understand his role. He could not see beyond today. It's not that his ideas were terrible; in fact, we later implemented many of them when the time was right. We were not going to try and launch into ten different ministries without the right team in place first. We were not going to do things halfway, just to say we did it. We were going to move and implement things when the time was right.

He finally saw what I was doing, and he trusted me enough to let things work out; soon, all of the things he wanted to do, we were doing; only we are doing them right.

So, within the local church, what makes a great team? Here are some principles of a great team.

1) UNITY

"But Peter, standing with the eleven, lifted up his

voice and addressed them..." (Acts 2:14 ESV)

As the Holy Ghost poured out, we see an incredible show of unity. They were ALL in one accord and in ONE mind. That's amazing. However, in verse 14, we see the results of a unified church. As Peter, anointed with the kingdom's keys, stands to deliver the first apostolic message in the New Testament church, the Bible says that the other 11 apostles stood with him. Why is that significant? Because a unified church will never allow the pastor to stand alone.

Peter's message was powerful because it was anointed. It was also powerful because it had the support of the body. If we want to develop a winning culture within the church, we need to learn to stand with our pastor and support him. I've seen too many Christians with what we call the pastor religion. I'll live right as long as the pastor can see. I'll be at church as long as the pastor is there. What would happen in our church and our homes if we changed our mindsets? If we showed up to the church and said, this isn't the pastor's church, this is MY church. This isn't the pastor's message; this is MY message.

I love what Luke writes in Acts 16. The Apostle Paul had a vision in the night; a man from Macedonia was pleading with him to come to them and help them. And Luke writes in Acts 16:10,

> *"AFTER HE had seen the vision, immediately we endeavored to go into Macedonia, assuredly gathering that the Lord had CALLED US for to preach the Gospel unto them."*

If we want to develop a winning culture within the church, we need to learn to stand with our pastor and support him.

followership

Luke and Timothy didn't have a vision; Paul did. Luke and Timothy weren't spiritual; they were asleep. Paul was seeking after God's will; he was trying to find the open door in the Spirit. Yet, Luke writes it like this: When God gave the pastor the vision, God called us to action.

We should stop making the ministry always validate their vision. Who cares how many days they've prayed and fasted over it? If God has given your church ministry a dream, it's not for you to decide if it's right or wrong. It's your job to stand with them. A unified church has a healthy balance of vision to action. Vision inspires action, and action inspires vision. Without vision, there can be no action, yet without action, there is no vision. In a healthy team, we need the visionaries to show us the way God is leading, and we need unity in action to do what God is calling us to do.

2) COMMITMENT

In 2 Samuel 15, Absalom had begun to deceive the hearts of God's people. And the Bible says Absalom stole the hearts of Israel. Guard your heart. The enemy wants nothing more than to steal your heart from the things of God. There's a reason the Bible says the heart is deceitful and wicked. You cannot discern your own heart. That's terrifying.

After stealing the hearts of Israel, Absalom devises a plan in which he would cause Israel to appoint him king over his father. David, to prevent anarchy, commanded his men to flee before Absalom could defeat them in the palace. The Bible says 600 men gathered with David outside the city. Among the 600 was a man named Ittai.

followership

> *"Then the king said to Ittai the Gittite, "Why do you also go with us? Go back and stay with the king, for you are a foreigner (it's not your job)and also an exile from your home. You came only yesterday (you're a new convert) and shall I today make you wander about with us, since I go I know not where? Go back and take your brothers with you, and may the Lord show steadfast love and faithfulness to you."*
> (2 Samuel 15:19-20 ESV)

Ittai, I appreciate your enthusiasm, but this isn't your responsibility, and you just started coming here. Go home and rest. Take it easy, and we'll pray that God continues to show you love and faithfulness.

Isn't this what we always do? We don't want to overwhelm our new converts or scare off our new people, so we, without really meaning to, discourage them from getting involved. Look at Ittai's response:

> *"But Ittai answered the king, 'As the Lord lives, and as my lord the king lives, wherever my lord the king shall be, whether for death or for life, there also will your servant be.'"* (2 Samuel 15:21 ESV)

Ittai says: As long as God is on the throne, and as long as you are my pastor, That's where I want to be. Whether it's to my benefit or not, where ever YOU are, that's where I want to be. It might not be my job, and it may not be my responsibility, but if it's important to you, pastor, it's important to me. I'm committed to helping the kingdom of God grow.

3) INVOLVEMENT

In Matthew 18, the disciples were trying to determine which of them was more significant than the next. So, one day they asked Jesus, "Jesus, who's the greatest in your kingdom."

> *"And calling to him a child, he put him in the midst of them and said, 'Truly, I say to you, unless you turn and become like children, you will never enter the kingdom of Heaven. Whoever humbles himself like this child is the greatest in the kingdom of Heaven.'"* (Matthew 18: 2-4 ESV)

Do you think that the disciples looked at each other and said, "oh yeah, that makes sense!" Probably not. They were probably left scratching their heads and saying, "a child?"

A few years ago, I had an old Chevy 1500, and the fuel pump had gone out on it. So my uncle came over to my house, took the bed of the truck off, and started changing the pump. In that truck, the fuel pump sat right on top of the fuel tank, making it easier to remove the bed than drop the fuel tank. Jaxson, my middle son, was probably five years old. He has always been one to want to help. So, he held the flashlight, but that wasn't enough. He would ask, *"Daddy, can I do that?" "Daddy, can I try that?" "Daddy, let me do that."*

When Mayli, my oldest daughter, and Jaxson were smaller, the question I got probably 100 times a day was, *"Daddy, what are you doing?" "Daddy, where are you going?" "Daddy, what are you eating?" "Daddy, I want some of that!"* Why? My kids never wanted to miss out on what daddy was doing.

Jesus said, unless we become like children, we will not make it to the kingdom of Heaven. It's time we set aside our petty pride and started acting like children. *"Pastor, can I try that?" "Pastor, let me do that!" "Pastor, what are you doing?" "Pastor, I want to try that!"* Let's find a way to get involved in the work of God.

chapter 3
- the flipside of leadership

Many have spent years studying the complex nature of leadership. Leadership is one of the most studied aspects of business, yet we still have many differing views. Perhaps the best way to understand leadership is to take the coin and flip it over.

The flipside of leadership is followership. If strong leadership is critical for success, then following is just as important: without followers, there are no leaders.

Historically, followership has been an understudied concept. As far back as 1933, management scholar Mary Parker Follett advocated for more research into a topic that she stated was "of the utmost importance, but which has been far too little considered, and that's the part of followers." Yet here we are, almost a century later, with still little research to show regarding followers.

Followership is what it is. It's the ability to follow—to take directions, run with them, get in line with the church's vision, willingly be a part of the team, and deliver what is expected of you. How well followers are at following determines how well leaders can lead.

followership

Unfortunately, followership has developed a bit of a bad rap. People are often labeled as weak, passive, or soft because they follow rather than lead. I can't begin to count the times a well-meaning leader would tell me to grow up and leave home simply because I was filling the role of a follower rather than the role of a leader.

Comments such as *"You're an excellent follower!"* are often backhanded compliments. Usually, the implication is, *"You don't have what it takes to lead."*

This attitude has become a real problem in the church world. We're raising future leaders who feel slighted when they are assigned positions of following rather than leading. The reality is that no one effectively climbs the leadership ladder without first demonstrating the ability to follow effectively. But we don't have much open discussion about this because following is not glamorous.

Our culture has downplayed the value of followership by placing the pinnacle of success upon leaders. Everyone is both a leader and a follower in one aspect or another, which only adds to the followership paradox.

One of the most outstanding leaders in all of the scripture wrote to the church in Corinth: *"Be ye followers of me, even as I also am of Christ"* (I Corinthians 11:1)

This statement's essence is excellent: Paul instructs the church to learn followership from his followership lifestyle.

When the Apostle Paul went about doing God's will, he never did it alone. With him, he always had young men following his example. Timothy, Titus, and others were just as relevant to the success of Paul's missionary journeys as

Great leaders are good
examples of great followers.

followership

he was.

If we want to revolutionize the concept of followership, we need to reevaluate our stereotypes concerning this discipline. We need to discover how effective followership can prepare us for effective leadership.

MISCONCEPTIONS ABOUT FOLLOWERSHIP

Leadership is more critical than followership.

The truth is this; followers give life to the vision of the leader. Without followers, the leader's dreams and aspirations are empty and useless. Influential followers validate the authority of leadership. Have you ever observed a leader who had no real power? Was it a result of his poor leadership? Could be. But it also could be the result of poor followership.

Strong followership always results in successful leadership.

Think for a moment: Was it Adolf Hitler's outstanding leadership that enabled Germany to sweep across Europe at will? Many historians consider Hitler to have been a poor leader. However, he was armed with what is now considered one of the most excellent military staff the world has ever seen.

For most of Hitler's time as Germany's chancellor, he allowed his knowledgeable military staff to strategize war plans. However, as Germany's influence and power increased, Hitler began to play, as the historians call it, "warlord." He began to disregard the strategy of those who had proven successful and instead began to make decisions independently.

Soon, Germany's ranks began to crumble as Hitler's blatant disregard for his followers led to an inevitable collapse of power. Many historians today consider the German regime to have had the potential for conquest. Many speculate they could've even won World War II if only Hitler had remained loyal to his followers.

Although we view the rise of the German regime through the lens of Hitler's leadership, the truth remains that followership, not leadership, created the German superpower.

Followers are followers because they don't have what it takes to lead.

This stigma is, unfortunately, commonly embraced in our culture. At times, during seasons when it was my ministry to sit behind my pastor rather than lead a church of my own, others questioned my ability to lead. Great leaders are not born in either secular and spiritual settings; they are developed through strong followership.

Aristotle once said, *"He who cannot be a good follower cannot be a good leader."* Profound, isn't it? Why is this true? Because the better you follow, the more you're able to learn.

Leadership requires knowledge, and most successful leaders didn't get where they are by reinventing the wheel. Instead of learning from scratch and blazing new trails, most leaders rely on the example of others who have shown outstanding leadership qualities, emulating them and building on what they learn.

I spent two years at Texas Bible College, gaining invaluable knowledge. However, the knowledge I gained there doesn't compare to the knowledge I gained working under my pastor for a decade. I watched him as he succeeded; I watched him through difficult seasons and during church conflicts. I've not attempted to create a ministry out of thin air; I'm building on what I've learned from him.

> *"If I have seen further than others, it is by standing upon the shoulders of giants."*
> -Sir Isaac Newton

Don't disregard the influence of your leaders. Learn from them, and then build on what you've learned. Your leadership journey will reach greater heights if you know to stand on the shoulders of those you follow.

The faster you learn, the quicker you accelerate the climb into leadership. For this reason, the most outstanding leaders of all time have prioritized finding a strong mentor early on in their careers.

As a young man, Warren Buffet famously knocked on the offices of renowned economist Benjamin Graham, literally harassing Mr. Graham to allow him to work under him—and for very little pay, at that. Warren spent nearly a decade under Mr. Graham's tutorship before setting up his first investment business.

Too often, people are looking for the overnight route to a leadership position. I've seen more than my share of

Leadership requires knowledge, and knowledge is gained through effective followership.

followership

young ministers "church hopping," looking for just the right job. In all this shuffling around for an advantage, they miss one critical foundation of leadership: EXPERIENCE.

Nobody wants to be a doctor's very first surgical patient. Nobody wants to trust their future to a financial advisor who's never traded on the stock market. In the same vein, no one wants a spiritual leader who has no corn in the crib!*

*Corn in the crib is an old cliché describing the process of harvesting corn. After the corn is collected from the fields, usually with the stalks still attached, the corn is placed in a corn house—a crib—to dry out and stay dry. Having corn in the crib means you've got credibility harvesting corn. Or, for this chapter, you have experience in ministry, and you have corn in the crib to prove it. You're welcome.

Experience is a beautiful thing. When I was an assistant pastor, I often told people that the most significant benefit of my position was that I learned how to be a pastor without pastoring! Isn't that great?

I like to compile lists of things I see in leaders I admire. These lists contain two critical components for how I'll lead in the future:

1. Things I Will Do

2. Things I Won't Do

I could have rushed the development process in my personal life and ambitiously sought a church to pastor before I was ready. But the reality is that I would've done more damage than good, both to myself and to the church I ended up pastoring.

There are some things you can learn only by experience. Just as no study can compare with hands-on experience living with a newborn baby, so will no amount of research prepare you for effective leadership. You need experience for that, and experience comes through a process of time and submission.

You can't just stand up and demand people follow you when you've never proven you can lead. People will trust experience over charisma every time. There's only one avenue to gain the knowledge you need: FOLLOWERSHIP.

chapter 4
- The Spiritual Life Cycle of a Follower

Babies are highly dependent on their parents. They grow and become less dependent, and as adults, most people have peer-like relationships with their parents.

Spiritual leadership and followership are much the same. Young Christians need routine care and attention from spiritual leaders. They need instruction, direction, and regular contact. They need assurance when they're doing well, correction when they err, and encouragement when they strive but fall short.

Mature Christians don't require their leadership to meet the same needs. They're well-schooled in basic instruction and don't need more. Having established themselves in maturity by living the Christian life experience (as we'll cover when we get into the book of Hebrews in a moment) they need a different type of relationship with leaders.

Returning to the human life analogy, do we expect a fourteen-year-old to ask the same questions as a three-year-old? How about when that teenager becomes a twenty-five-year-old? Do we give them the same answers and keys to success we did when they were a three-year-

Trouble brews when leaders and followers ignore the life cycle reality of leadership/followership.

followership

old? How absurd!

Jesus treated the apostles one way as they began following Him, and another way as they matured. (We'll cover this more in a moment.) There is a large body of scriptural evidence on the topic of spiritual life cycles.

As a three children parent, I have seen that it's hard for children to grow up. It's also hard for parents to adjust to their children growing up. What makes the process more manageable is realizing that there are different stages along the way and that growth from phase to phase is a natural process.

Leaders and followers would do well to apply lessons from physical life to spiritual life. If we understand the growth dynamic of new and mature Christians, we are more likely to have a healthy and beneficial leadership/ followership experience.

Let's examine this theory through the lens of scripture. Jesus spoke of the life cycle of faith in Matthew 18 as the people pressed Him with the question, "Who is the greatest in the kingdom?"

Jesus then called for a child and made this statement:

"Verily I say unto you, Except ye be converted, and become as little children, ye shall not enter into the kingdom of heaven" (Matthew 18:3)

Most of the time, we mistake this text to mean that Jesus wants us to be like and stay like children. However, the context of this passage revolves around conversion. There is a reason we refer to conversion as being "born again."

After conversion, life begins all over again—not physically, but spiritually. You start in the infant stage and develop as a child does. When Jesus gave this statement, He didn't intend for us to stay like children; He intended for us to develop like children.

> *"For every one that useth milk is unskillful in the word of righteousness: for he is a babe. But strong meat belongeth to them that are of full age, even those who by reason of use have their senses exercised to discern both good and evil"* (Hebrews 5:13-14)

The NIV says it this way:

> *"Anyone who lives on milk, being still an infant, is not acquainted with the teaching about righteousness. But solid food is for the mature, who by constant use have trained themselves to distinguish good from evil."*

Essentially, if you are an infant, we don't expect you to digest the meat of the Word. We hope you to feed off the milk. You don't get the Holy Ghost and understand the principles of righteousness immediately. But as with nature, so also should the child of God experience healthy spiritual development.

Just as natural development takes time, trial, and error, spiritual growth requires patience and diligence. You can also expect mistakes along the way.

Let me drive this point home: You must train yourself to

He didn't intend for us to stay like children; He intended for us to develop like children.

followership

distinguish between good and evil. The above passage from Hebrews in the King James Version says, *"your spiritual senses should be exercised to discern good from evil."*

You must train yourself to be spiritual. This training requires spending time in prayer, searching the Word, and being faithful to church. Your spirit needs regular workouts that build up spiritual strength for discerning good from evil.

There's a reason we don't crucify new converts over specific issues, yet we expect seasoned saints to know better. It's not that we have a double-standard; it's that we recognize the different stages of development among God's children.

Jesus exemplified this principle with His disciples. When He found them, they began their life as spiritual babes. They weren't yet the twelve apostles; they were the twelve servants.

Jesus told an interesting parable in Luke 17 ESV:

"Will any one of you who has a servant plowing or keeping sheep say to him when he has come in from the field, 'Come at once and recline at table'? Will he not rather say to him, 'Prepare supper for me, and dress properly, and serve me while I eat and drink, and afterward you will eat and drink'? Does he thank the servant because he did what was commanded? So you also, when you have done all that you were commanded, say, 'We are unworthy servants; we have only done what was our duty.'"

Reading this from the context of our culture makes it

seem like a harsh and heartless conversation. But service was a real occupation in those days. The point Jesus drove home was that being a servant is a thankless job.

Many people come to Jesus with a misconception that God blesses you for doing right. That couldn't be further from the truth. The reality is that God blesses you because He's good. Often, immature Christians get upset with God when they do good, and it doesn't seem God is blessing them for it. What Jesus was trying to convey to His disciples is that you have only done what is expected of you by doing good.

It's no wonder the Bible says to present our bodies a living sacrifice, holy and acceptable unto the Lord: this is our reasonable service.

Don't expect the windows of Heaven to open when you live holy. As a Christian, righteous living is your duty. We need to restructure our mentality when it comes to blessings.

We don't get blessed because of what we do; we get blessed because of who God is!

Jesus reinforced this principle when Zebedee's wife came to Him and requested that her two sons sit one on the right hand of Him, and the other on the left. You have to understand the context of this to grasp what is transpiring. Zebedee was a wealthy man. It is believed that Zebedee might have financed the ministry of Jesus.

Zebedee's sons, James and John, were disciples of Jesus. Mark 3:17 says Jesus nicknamed these brothers the "sons of thunder," meaning they were given to "thunderings": they were dangerous. Jesus knew these boys had the

We don't get blessed because
of what we do; we get blessed
because of who God is!

followership

potential to think too highly of themselves.

Sure enough, here they are, wanting to be as junior gods in Heaven. These brothers thought that since their father had given so much money to Jesus, they had earned elite status. Jesus responded, *"Are you willing to drink from the same cup I will drink from?"* They said yes, but Jesus knew better.

This scene caused friction between these two pompous brothers and the other ten disciples. Catch this; it's fascinating: The rest of the ten disciples were angry because they didn't like the idea of being somehow inferior to James and John. It certainly wasn't humility that caused the dispute. Deep down, the other ten wanted to be the greatest in the kingdom, too! These men were still young Christ-followers, which we often forget as we read the gospels.

> *"But Jesus called them to him and said, 'You know that the rulers of the Gentiles lord it over them, and their great ones exercise authority over them. It shall not be so among you. But whoever would be great among you must be your servant, and whoever would be first among you must be your slave, even as the Son of Man came not to be served but to serve, and to give his life as a ransom for many'"* (Matthew 20:25-28)

In the world's kingdoms, the greater you are, the more you rule. It's not that way in God's kingdom. If you want to be great, you must be a servant. Jesus said, *"Look to my example. I didn't come to be 'somebody'; I came to serve and to give my life a ransom for many."*

followership

The first stage of spiritual development is the servant stage. When they start going to church, many people believe that the church is there to serve them. That's not how Jesus created this thing to work.

The church doesn't serve you; you serve the church.

That doesn't mean that the ministry isn't there for you—we most assuredly are. But it does mean that you aren't in the church to be a consumer; you are there to serve. If we want to grow in Christ, we must be willing to serve.

In Philippians 2, the Apostle Paul addressed critical principles in the development of followership.

1) BE AGREEABLE.

The Greek word phroneo means not to let one's opinion of himself exceed the bounds of modesty. Another translation is *"to cherish the views or the opinions of another."* In other words, avoid the temptation to think you have all the answers.

Being agreeable doesn't mean you're a yes-man; it means you're open to others' ideas and that you don't push and promote your own.

This is one of the biggest hurdles to followership development. We tend to value our ideas over the ideas of everyone else.

Learn to hear people out. Be slow to chime in; allow others to voice their ideas, even if you're sure you know better. Have a cooperative spirit.

2) WORK TOGETHER IN UNITY.

In Philippians 2, Paul uses a familiar word when he instructs believers to be in one accord. The Greek word used is sympsychos (soom'-psoo-khos) It is made up of two words: sun (soon) meaning "together/with," and psuchos, meaning "soul, self, inner life, etc." The word itself refers to being united in spirit.

Paul implored the Ephesian church to endeavor to keep the unity of the Spirit (Ephesians 4:3)

What he meant wasn't that they should keep a spirit of unity, but rather that they should be unified with the Spirit. This is critical in spiritual development. We may not see eye to eye, but we must stay unified with the Spirit of God.

In Acts 2, the 120 souls in the upper room weren't strategizing their revival; they were in one accord. They were unified with the Spirit. So when the Holy Ghost fell, they all received the Holy Ghost.

We need to be unified not just with each other, but collectively, with the Spirit.

3) BE SELFLESS.

Paul said in Philippians 2:3, *"Let nothing be done through strife or vainglory."*

The word "strife" in Greek is the word eritheia, meaning "to be given to electioneering or intriguing for office. A desire to put one's self forward."

In Greek culture, this word is found before the New

Testament era only during Aristotle's life, denoting the self-seeking pursuit of political office by unfair means.

Essentially, what Paul was dealing with here was a spirit in which people were trying to manipulate situations to their advantage and weasel themselves into positions via unethical means.

The word "vainglory" comes from the Greek word kenodoxia, meaning "glorying without reason," or being vain for nothing.

It's incredible how many people think they've had something to do with their call and their successes in ministry. When you take credit for anything God does, that's vainglory. When you take credit for a group project, that's vainglory. When you try and make everything about you, that's vainglory.

4) BE HUMBLE.

"But in lowliness of mind let each other esteem other better than themselves" (Philippians 2:3)

To esteem means to lead or give authority. In other words, you should be happy when other people have an opportunity to lead. A maturing follower's sign is their willingness to let others take the lead—not abandoning their responsibilities but enabling others' leadership.

5) DON'T BE SELF-ABSORBED. FOCUS ON OTHERS.

Don't be so consumed with your own life and struggles that you miss opportunities to minister to others.

6) UNDERSTAND CHRIST'S HUMILITY.

I love the wording of Philippians 2:5-11 in the English Standard Version:

"Have this mind among yourselves, which is yours in Christ Jesus, who, though he was in the form of God, did not count equality with God a thing to be grasped, but emptied himself, by taking the form of a servant, being born in the likeness of men. And being found in human form, he humbled himself by becoming obedient to the point of death, even death on a cross. Therefore God has highly exalted him and bestowed on him the name that is above every name, so that at the name of Jesus every knee should bow, in Heaven and on earth and under the earth, and every tongue confess that Jesus Christ is Lord, to the glory of God the Father."

Here's where Paul tries to connect the believer's development and maturity to the mind that was in Christ. Paul stressed some critical elements of followership: the agreeable spirit, unity, selflessness, humility, and being mindful of others.

These are all areas in which Jesus' disciples struggled. Peter, for instance, did not have a cooperative spirit. At one point, Peter even rebuked Jesus, disagreeing with what He was saying.

Earlier, I told of how Zebedee's sons allowed

themselves to get proud, causing friction among the disciples through strife and vainglory. This situation was the epitome of vainglory, as they assumed that since their father was wealthy and contributed much to Jesus' ministry, they deserved a position.

Humanity, since the fall in Eden, has always struggled with this thing called flesh.

In Philippians 2, Paul wasn't just making a list of things to preach about; he identified areas of greatest need where personal growth is concerned. Here, he depicted the spirit of a mature believer based on Christ's example.

Adam allowed his position in God's creation to make him prideful, so he reached and grasped something that didn't belong to him. Jesus, however, took off His royal splendor and took upon Himself the form of a servant. He did not count equality with God a thing to be grasped.

Although Christ was God robed in the flesh, He willingly laid down His crown in favor of a towel.

Where Adam was lifted up in pride, Jesus stooped down in humility.

This mind—this attitude—needs to be in every believer. As we develop maturity in our relationship with God, we should become more like Him. The more we grow, the more we should serve.

7) DON'T COMPLAIN OR ARGUE.

"For it is God which worketh in you both to will and to do of His good pleasure. Do all things without murmurings and disputings" (Philippians 2:13-14)

God wants you to develop and grow in Him because He's trying to work something in you so that He can then work through you.

He's working on you for His good pleasure. So don't complain or argue about what is required of you. Do it happily.

WHY IS THAT IMPORTANT?

"That you may be blameless and innocent, children of God without blemish in the midst of a crooked and twisted generation, among whom you shine as lights in the world" (Philippians 2:15)

As Paul concludes these principles, he begins to speak about Timothy. I love how Paul does this: He's just laid out a blueprint for Christian development, and he's explained that the most significant position to seek after is that of service. Now he says, *"I'm sending Timothy to you, for I have no man likeminded."* Or better yet, "I have no man who is like me: he's so much like me that he will naturally care for you. Most young men are only interested in themselves, not in what is Christ's. Yet you know how Timothy, like a son to his father, has served me in the gospel."

Paul also felt it was necessary to send Epaphroditus, his brother, companion in labor, and fellow soldier "because for the work of Christ he was nigh unto death, not regarding his life, to supply your lack of service toward me."

The Philippian church sent Epaphroditus to serve Paul during his missionary trip. While serving Paul, he got sick—so sick that he almost died. Because Epaphroditus was so dedicated to service, however, he disregarded his wellbeing to make sure his man of God was being tended to.

Epaphroditus was a young man, but he willingly risked his life to serve Paul. This dedication is the spirit of followowership Paul is trying to portray in this second chapter of Philippians.

Service is the most significant element of followowership you can possess.

Let's take the principle of service even further.

Isaiah said in Isaiah 40:31, *"But they that wait upon the Lord shall renew their strength; they shall mount up with wings as eagles; they shall run and not be weary; and they shall walk, and faint not."*

That word "wait" doesn't mean to sit around until God does something. It means "to wait on" as a server would wait on someone. It means to serve. Those who regard God over themselves even in weakness are the ones whose strength shall be renewed.

When you look at this verse, it at first appears the sequence is out of order. How do you fly, then run, then walk? Shouldn't you have to learn how to walk, then transition that walk into running, and then finally, once you can run, fly like an eagle?

It might make more sense if this were a physical process, but it's a spiritual one.

How do these elements apply to us spiritually?

1)   Fly   1)   Elevation
2)   Run   2)   Acceleration
3)   Walk   3)   Determination

Service is the most significant element of followership you can possess.

followership

followership

This is the developmental process for followers. As you serve God, you will experience SPIRITUAL ELEVATION as God takes you to places you've never been.

You will then experience SPIRITUAL ACCELERATION. Suddenly, things will begin to make sense, and your knowledge and understanding will rapidly increase.

Finally, you will experience SPIRITUAL DETERMINATION. This is where it doesn't matter what comes against you or what tries to destroy you: your mind is made up, and you will continue to serve God. God expects each of us to mature into spiritually determined followers.

> *"Ye are my friends, if ye do whatsoever I command you. Henceforth I call you not servants; for the servant knoweth not what his Lord doeth: but I have called you friends; for all things that I have heard of my Father I have made known unto you"* (John 15:14-15)

Here, Jesus is preparing His disciples for life without Him. They have passed the tests of development. They are dedicated and determined to serve Jesus to the death. Now, Jesus looks at them and says, *"You are my friends as long as you keep my commands. From this day forward, I won't call you servants any longer, because servants don't know what the master is doing. I'm now calling you friends, because everything I have heard from Heaven, I've given you."*

Then Jesus says, *"Ye have not chosen me, but I have chosen you, and ordained you, that ye should go and bring forth fruit, and that your fruit should remain: that whatsoever ye shall ask of the Father in my name, he may give it you"* (John 15:16)

The ask-and-you-shall-receive principle is contingent upon your maturity development. Jesus said, *"I didn't just call you to have fruit; I called you so that your fruit would remain. This isn't a seasonal blessing, and I expect you to develop your relationship to a place where you can ask me anything, and I'll do it."*

I call this the friend zone!

Our culture uses this phrase with a negative connotation. In the world, if you're pursuing a relationship and get stuck in the friend zone, it's not a good thing. However, when it comes to our relationship with God, we desire to make our way into the friend zone!

There is only one man in scripture, discounting what Jesus said to Judas in the garden (I won't get into that in this book) that God ever called a friend.

> *"And the scripture was fulfilled which saith, Abraham believed God, and it was imputed unto him for righteousness: and he was called the Friend of God"* (James 2:23)

In Isaiah 41:8, God Himself gave Abraham this title: *"But thou, Israel, art my servant, Jacob whom I have chosen, the seed of Abraham my friend."*

Abraham believed God. He blindly followed God out of his homeland. He trusted in God. Hebrews 11:8 says, *"By faith Abraham, when he was called to go out into a place which he should after receive for an inheritance, obeyed; and he went out, not knowing whither he went."*

Verses 17 through 19 say, *"By faith Abraham, when he was tried, offered up Isaac: and he that had received the promises offered up his only begotten son, Of whom it was said, That in Isaac shall thy seed be called: Accounting that God was able to raise him up, even from the dead; from whence also he received him in a figure."*

The English Standard Version says it this way: *"He considered that God was able even to raise him from the dead, from which, figuratively speaking, he did receive him back"* (11:19)

Think about the faith Abraham had in God. He knew that God had spoken a promise over Isaac. He said, "Even if God makes me kill him, God will raise him from the dead! Even if I let him go now, God will raise him up later."

However, as Abraham led Isaac up the mountain one way, God led provision up another way. By the time Abraham was ready to make the sacrifice, God already had a provision waiting on him.

God told Abraham, *"Because of your unwavering faith, you aren't a servant any longer. You are my friend!"*

SO WHAT DOES THAT MEAN EXACTLY?

When Lot was in Sodom, God told Abraham what His plan was, and Abraham negotiated with God. When you are in the friend zone, you have a connection with God where He lets you in on what He's doing—and you are close enough to Him to intercede for those who are lost!

Here's what's fascinating and gets me excited:

In John 8:56, speaking to the Pharisees, Jesus said, *"Your father Abraham rejoiced to see my day: and he saw it, and was glad."*

Wait—Abraham never saw God! When did Abraham see this day?

Let's go back to Genesis. As they prepare for the sacrifice, Isaac tells his father, *"I see the wood and the tools, but where's the sacrifice?"*

Abraham responds prophetically in Genesis 22:8: *"My son, God will provide himself a lamb for a burnt offering."*

I don't know if Abraham fully grasped what he was saying, but I have to believe that in the time after they left Mt. Sinai, God let Abraham in on a little secret. Remember, Jesus said, *"We are friends because everything I have heard from my father, have I disclosed to you!"*

It's the life cycle of a follower—the development from infancy to maturity. God wants to transition you from the new convert stage, to the servant stage, to the friend zone.

As Moses saw a seemingly insignificant bush, ignited by God's flame, he witnessed a miracle. Yet speaking loudly from within the embers that lit that bush on fire, was the reality that God could take something insignificant and turn it into a miracle. That bush was a picture of what God had planned to do with Moses; he was the weak bush, but God was the empowering fire, and with God's help, Moses was about to find out that he could accomplish anything!

When the Apostle Paul wrote to the Philippian church and said, *"I can do all things through Christ, which strengtheneth me."* The word he used for strength is the Greek word en-doo-nam-o'-o meaning to empower. What Paul was saying is exactly what God was trying to tell Moses. I may be weak and insignificant, but through God's spirit, I can do anything. Because it's not me that does it, it's His spirit that empowers.

As Moses beheld the bush, the Bible says God spoke to Moses. It's here we find an interesting exchange as God commands Moses to take off his shoes, for the ground in which he stands in holy.

I wondered why God would make such a request of Moses. Only one other time in scripture would God make such a request, and that would be 80 years from now when the Lord would appear and tell Joshua, in Joshua 5:15, to take off his shoes as well.

I believe there are two fundamental reasons why this event took place. First, in ancient Jewish customs, the removal of the shoe signified the transfer of ownership. If I were to sell or give ownership of my land, I would remove my shoe to show that I relinquish my rights to that land.

Here's the first thing God was telling Moses, Moses, I need you to relinquish control of your life to me. Here's the thing, God said, do not come near me unless you are willing to remove your shoes.

The first thing we have to do when we come to God is to relinquish our lives to Him.

There was another reason, though. The removal of the shoe indicated that the person removing their shoe was either unwilling to redeem or merely unable to redeem.

Understand the context of this burning bush experience. God is about to commission Moses to redeem His people from Egypt. Yet, before God commands Moses to redeem, He tells Moses to remove His shoes. Moses, I'm about to call you to do something that you are incapable of doing. That's what God was saying.

God wasn't trying to insult or belittle Moses. He was trying to get Moses to be humble. See, there is a difference between humility and inferiority.

Humility understands that God is the only one with the power. Humble people will be capable because they know it's not their ability; it's God's. Humble people recognize that they couldn't do what they're doing without God. Humble people understand that if 50 people pray through tomorrow, it wasn't because of anything the church did, it's because of what God did.

Inferiority is different. People who deal with inferiority complexes believe that God won't because they can't. Big difference. The enemy wants to imprison you in your inferiority. For forty years, Moses lived in mediocrity. He thought that he failed and assumed it was because he wasn't cut out for it. God has shown up, speaking to Moses from a burning bush, and Moses is arguing with God. Moses is telling God, this will never work, because I can't do that.

God is saying this, Moses; you don't understand; that's precisely why this will work. God wasn't insulting Moses; he was trying to give Moses a revelation.

Moses, you will become a mighty deliverer to my people, you will walk into Egypt, and you will redeem my people. I want you to know from the beginning; you cannot do this on your own. You tried it your way once before, and now you've spent the last forty years running from your mistakes. Moses, you can't redeem them. That's the whole point - but I will be with you!

When you walk into Egypt and look the most powerful ruler in the face, understand Moses, it's not you that's speaking to him, it's me.

followership

Something exciting happens next. God said, I have seen their affliction; I have heard their cry, and I have come to deliver them. Then God says in Exodus 3:10, *"Come, I will send you to Pharaoh that you may bring my people the children of Israel out of Egypt. But Moses said to God, who am I that I should go to Pharaoh...?"*

There are two powerful principles that God is revealing through this encounter with Moses at the burning bush. First, Moses asked God, *"Who am I?"*

I'm a lonely, misfit shepherd who's spent the last forty years running from all my problems. Why would I go to Pharaoh? Here's where my imagination kicks in, I'm sure Moses was like, *"I thought you saw, heard, and had come to deliver them? If so, then why am I going?"* As Moses was trying to get a grip on what God was calling him to do, the question that filled his head, was *"Who am I?"*

At one time, Moses thought he was able to deliver Israel from their oppression. He felt that he would have the influence and resources to make it happen because he was in Egypt. As a result, Moses acted too hastily. Now, he's spent forty years wandering the backside of a mountain, and he knows full well the limitations of his weakness. The more you learn about God and yourself, the more aware you are of your flaws and weaknesses.

Before we can go any further, we must be honest with ourselves. When I was a Pastor, the greatest, yet most challenging lesson I ever learned was that I was not equipped to lead my church. That wasn't necessarily a bad thing. The weight of responsibility and the pressure to be charismatic and entertaining while also remaining profoundly spiritual and enlightening can be debilitating. However, my biggest enemy is myself. Through various circumstances in my life, I have deep insecurities.

Because of these deep insecurities, I feel the need to "prove" myself at every turn. That's dangerous. Because of this chip on my shoulder, I can't show weakness. This chip leads to me focusing too much time and energy into things I'm not good at because I'm afraid if people see my flaws, they'll no longer feel the same way about me.

> "Devoting a little of yourself to everything means committing a great deal of yourself to nothing."

As a pastor, if I focused on tasks outside of my strengths, I realize the negative impact this can have on the momentum and the focus of the whole church. I had to learn to be open and transparent about my weaknesses because my flaws are another person's opportunity.

I love the way the writer of Hebrews depicts Jacob. There's no account given of his epic wrestling match with an angel. No emphasis on his exploits, his heritage, or his pedigree. Yet, in the chapter full of heroic icons and heroic feats, scripture says in Hebrews 11:21 (NLT) *"It was by faith that Jacob, when he was old and dying, blessed each of Joseph's sons and bowed in worship as he leaned on his staff."*

What does Hebrews record as Jacob's heroic act? Being weak and feeble, leaning on his staff? The only reason Jacob has a staff is that his hip was dislodged, and he struggles walking. Jacob, by faith, embraced his weakness. When Jacob embraced his vulnerability, God was able to use Him for His purpose.

followership

I can't lead a church, at least not on my own. I've learned to embrace my weaknesses so that the team that God has placed around me can be empowered, and the church can succeed.

There was something else Moses had to learn as well. It wasn't good enough to understand his weakness. Before his exile from Egypt as a criminal, Moses had a healthy dose of self-confidence mingled with strong faith and zeal. Now, a sinful distrust has crept in under the guise of humility. Moses wasn't humble; Moses revealed that his understanding of his weaknesses had caused him to lose trust in God's ability to use him. Moses couldn't separate God's call from his inadequacies. So, rather than pursuing God's call with the same youthful zeal he did forty years prior, Moses is now reluctant to believe that God could use him.

So, God had to give Moses the I AM revelation. Moses, before you try to write this whole mission off because of your weaknesses, let me let you in on a little secret. While Moses was trying to figure out the mystery of "AM I," God gave him a revelation of "I AM."

No, Moses, you are not supposed to do this. I AM! That's the whole point. It was never about you, it's always been about me! No, Moses, you aren't walking into Pharaoh's courts, I AM!

"...I will be with you..."

When you walk into Pharaoh's courts, it won't be you walking in there; it's going to be me walking there. When you open your mouth and speak to Pharaoh, it won't be your words you speak; it will be my words. Moses, you're going, but I'm going with you.

Moses, I AM has sent you. Do you know what God was saying? Moses, I AM. Therefore, by definition, you are not. It wasn't an insult as much as it was a reminder. I'm the all-powerful one; you are not. I'm the deliverer; you are not. I'm the healer; you are not. I'm the redeemer; you are not. Before you think that this is impossible, understand this isn't about you – it's about ME.

There will always be a struggle between the reality of who "I AM," and the revelation of "I AM."

The reality of who "AM I" reveals the weaknesses and the limitations that prove I can't do this.

The revelation of "I AM" shows that it was never about my strength or ability; it's about His strength, His power, and His purpose. When I embrace the reality of who I am and relinquish control under the revelation of who He is, suddenly, God empowers me to do His will.

chapter 5
- the impact of a follower

"And he saith unto them, Follow me, and I will make you fishers of men." (Matthew 4:19)

Jesus called His disciples not to occupy significant positions or hold essential titles, but to follow a man and His cause. Their obedience to that call took ordinary fishermen and transformed them into the fathers of the Christian faith.

The disciples' choice to follow Jesus allowed them to be taught by Him and see the great miracles He did. Because the disciples chose to follow Christ, others later made that same choice as they saw Jesus in these men.

As the New Testament church was gaining momentum, Peter and John, on their way to the temple to pray, found a lame man at the gate called Beautiful. The Bible says this man was there daily begging for alms.

Peter and John laid hands on him, and he was miraculously healed. As people celebrated this miracle, the religious council brought Peter and John in and questioned them. By what authority, they demanded, was this man healed?

"Then Peter, filled with the Holy Spirit, said to them, 'Rulers of the people and elders, if we are being examined today concerning a good deed done to a crippled man, by what means this man has been healed, let it be known to all of you and to all the people of Israel that by the name of Jesus Christ of Nazareth, whom you crucified, whom God raised from the dead—by him this man is standing before you well. This Jesus is the stone that was rejected by you, the builders, which has become the cornerstone. And there is salvation in no one else, for there is no other name under Heaven given among men by which we must be saved.' Now when they saw the boldness of Peter and John, and perceived that they were uneducated, common men, they were astonished. And they recognized that they had been with Jesus" (Acts 4:8-13 ESV)*

Notice, it wasn't the miraculous demonstration that convinced the Pharisees that Peter and John had been with Jesus. It was their response.

One, these men appeared to have an incredible grasp of Old Testament theology. Two, they had an even more excellent grasp of Christ in Old Testament theology. It didn't make sense to the proud, educated theologians who made up this ministerial committee of Pharisees. Peter and John were uneducated and common men.

It won't be our miracles that prove to the world our experience with Jesus Christ: it will be our excellent understanding of who He is.

Jesus Christ must be the One you follow first and foremost. His image must be the mark you see in the

Notice, it wasn't the miraculous demonstration that convinced the Pharisees that Peter and John had been with Jesus. It was their response.

followership

followership

Christian leaders you choose to follow.

The Apostle Paul told his followers in I Corinthians 11:1: *"Be ye followers of me, even as I also am of Christ." The ESV says it this way: "Be imitators of me, as I am of Christ."*

Leadership is required to emulate Christ in such a way that their followers will not be following man's charisma, but Christ's character.

It has been said that followership is the doorway to the workshop where future leaders are made. Following is an opportunity to open oneself to godly and faithful mentors who will one day hand over the baton of leadership. It is a call to learn from the wisdom and the mistakes of those who have gone before us.

I know that some of you want to change the world right now. You want to influence people positively with great ideas and passion. But God is never in a hurry. The greatest mistake you will ever make is to think you can bypass growth today and expect to influence others tomorrow.

Jesus Christ, who came to the world, knowing what He had to do, still sat under Joseph and Mary's guidance and asked questions at the temple. In the same way, God has placed godly people and institutions in your path for a reason. To ignore them is to ignore God's process for making you the leader He intends you to be.

Some of you, however, may be hesitant to become leaders. You think you will never be good enough, never be strong enough, and never know the Scriptures well enough. You are quite willing to let leadership do all the leading. You'd like to remain a follower all your life. But real followers are those who grow, develop, and are willing to

Leadership is required to emulate Christ in such a way that their followers will not be following man's charisma, but Christ's character.

followership

take the next risky steps toward responsible leadership.

The enemy knows that God can turn ordinary fishermen into fishers of men. He knows that a Simon who chooses to follow can become a Peter who will obey God rather than fear men. He knows that a prostitute like Mary Magdalene can become a follower of Jesus and turn into someone worthy to be entrusted with the first resurrection news of Jesus Christ. He is aware that godly leaders, like Timothy's mentor, Paul, will encourage you to fan into flame the gift of God in you so that you will be able to counter false teachers.

So the enemy launches an aggressive attack aimed at convincing followers that they were created to follow and nothing else.

I don't care who you are; God never calls anyone to fill up space on a pew. God calls His people to go and make disciples—or better yet, to go and develop followers! There is a life cycle of development: followers grow, develop, begin to assume the lead, and then go out to help others develop into leaders.

You may never fill a ministerial office or a leadership position on the church staff, but you are still called to be a leader in our world.

Followership needs the right kind of leadership. Good leaders are not those who do everything themselves. Good leaders don't try to maintain total control, nor do they delight in the power and prestige that sometimes comes with leadership. Instead, they model stable leadership while standing behind their followers and encouraging them to take the lead. They are happy to see others grow up to take their place: they are always looking for those who can carry on the work without them.

True leaders emulate the leadership and development methods of the Apostle Paul. While doing work in Corinth, Paul found a couple named Aquila and Priscilla. The Bible says they were tentmakers like Paul, so he stayed and developed a relationship with them.

That's the first step in impacting the lives of others: friendship. Abraham Lincoln once said, "If you are to win a man to your cause, you must first convince him that you are his sincere friend."

After Paul developed a friendship with this couple, he offered them an opportunity to serve with him. This is the next stage: showing people that you trust them to work alongside you. Get people involved; make them feel as if they have something to offer.

We don't need leaders who perceive themselves as godsends. We don't need leaders who will alienate potential followers by making leadership all about them. Good leaders enlist the help of people who are there to serve.

Along with offering Aquila and Priscilla an opportunity to work with him, Paul invested in them as peers. He equipped them with knowledge and resources to enable them to succeed.

We need to become an equipping church. We can't be a church of one or two people doing everything. We need the maturity to develop people from the front door to the back door and everywhere in between. Invest in people, equip people, and prepare people to be ready to lead.

After investing in them, Paul left Aquila and Priscilla in Ephesus for two years to plant a church. It should be the goal of every leader to inspire, invest, and release. If we want sustainable growth, we need leaders producing leaders. That happens only through sustained followership.

Daniel Bourdanné, IFES (International Fellowship of Evangelical Students) general secretary, made this clear when he took over leadership of IFES in 2007. In his inaugural talk, he said,

> *"It is not for nothing that we underline in our fellowship the initiative of students, because it is when they work themselves that they learn, through their failures and their successes, to become future leaders. We need to encourage students; we need to leave them room on the campus so that they take initiative for their Bible studies, for their training camps. The staff should be there to encourage them and support them, but not to work in their places. I realize, dear brothers and sisters, that the trend sometimes in some of our movements is to focus too much on the staff. We must put our emphasis on student initiative, on the commitment of students to the work of evangelism."*

More recently, in response to a question from World Student Day 2012, Bourdanné added,

> *"You can easily kill the dynamic of a student movement by being staff-led rather than student-led. If staff are doing it all, it is not helping students to grow. Some staff are afraid of the failures and the mistakes students can make; they tend to do everything themselves. This doesn't help students to learn from their failures and mistakes and to grow as disciples. But it is also not healthy if there are no staff to work alongside the students, to model and pray for and*

support them pastorally."

A letter to IFES students concludes,

"God has helped your leaders to put together programs that will help you grow into Christ-likeness. Enter into them with enthusiasm and joy! You are a gift to the next generation but also to your own generation. Choose today to learn leadership through following Jesus' followers."

I love this so much! Daniel Bourdanné set his students up for success by recognizing the impact they could make. He understood that if the students developed a leadership-dependent mentality, it would dwarf their growth. He intentionally encouraged an atmosphere in which the students weren't dependent on the staff for the school's success—rather an atmosphere in which the students were the driving force of success.

Allow me to explain why this approach is biblically supported:

In Joel 2:28, the prophet prophesies, *"And it shall come to pass afterward, that I will pour out my spirit upon all flesh; and your sons and your daughters shall prophesy, your old men shall dream dreams, your young men shall see visions."*

Joel prophesies of the outpouring of the Holy Ghost. He sees old men having dreams and young men having visions. In Hebrew, the word that Joel uses for "dream" is the Hebrew word chalam, meaning "to bind firmly in hand."

The word he uses for "visions" is the Hebrew word

chizzayown, meaning "a revelation that comes by a dream." Another translation says, "to look and learn."

When Joel saw the church of the last days, he saw a church where the elders had a grasp of truth and in which young men watched. It was the older men who empowered young men. Joel saw an elder-dependent church.

When Joel looked at the last days' church, he saw a church where the elders did everything. Joel spoke of strong elders who had an incredible grasp of this thing.

I don't know about you, but I'm thankful for the men and women who blazed this trail for us. I'm grateful for every elder who took an unpopular stand and defended the truth even when it wasn't easy. I'm thankful for the men and women who refused to let go of this message regardless of the battles they had to fight. Without their resiliency, we wouldn't be here today.

In Acts 2, Joel's prophecy comes to pass. The Holy Ghost falls, and Peter recites the prophecy: *"And it shall come to pass in the last days, saith God, I will pour out of my Spirit upon all flesh: and your sons and your daughters shall prophesy, and your young men shall see visions, and your old men shall dream dreams'"* (Acts 2:17)

It at first appears as if Peter has misrepresented Joel's prophecy. Peter rearranges the order of the young men and the old men!

The word Peter uses for "dream" is the Greek word hypnos, meaning "mental or physical inactivity due to weariness." Peter is not speaking of lazy elders. He is speaking of elders who are mentally and physically fatigued.

I believe we have been an elder/leader-dependent

movement for too long, and I've spoken to elders who will vouch for it. We have leaned on them so long that we have just about killed them.

Moses was the leader of the children of Israel. Moses understood his position's responsibility, and he knew that his hands were responsible for the victory. Yet, in the middle of battle, Moses got tired.

We need to understand; it's not a sin for a leader to become weary.

We need strong leaders—but when the leaders are the only ones praying, their hands will become heavy.

The Effect of Weary Elders

In Lamentations 5, the Bible begins to paint a picture that resembles that of Ezekiel 22 vividly. This time coming from the perspective of those living in it. It chronicles the sin and the perversion among the people, and it begins to sum up the entire condition of Israel in verses 12-15. The Bible says that they hung the princes and nobles by their hands, and the elders were no longer honored. They forced the young men to carry grinding stones, and they stumbled and fell under loads of wood. Each generation was facing circumstances that were unique to the other generation.

The result of this unfortunate season is that the elders ceased from the gates, and the young men ceased from their music, and joy left their hearts, and the dancing of the people turned to mourn.

Due to the world around them and the years spent serving, the elders became weary at the gates. The young

It's not a sin for a leader to become weary.

followership

men became weary by the burden of carrying the load, and so they lost their desire to play music.

In the book of Lamentations, we see the effects of weary elders: The elders have lost their purpose. The result? The next generation lost their passion. When the elders lose their purpose, and the young people lose their passion, the church loses its promise.

I am afraid that Satan has launched an all-out war against the people of God, a subtle yet, deadly war. He has successfully divided generations. I'm worried that this is where we are as a collective church.

There is a divide between the elders and the younger generation. There's a gap in our movement. Hell is fighting the elders, distracting them from their purpose, and he's fighting young men and women, diverting them from their passion. Yet, we can't discern it as war. Instead, we think it's merely a result of culture or generational differences when in reality, Satan has been tormenting the minds of elders and telling them that they can no longer do what they used to do. Therefore they no longer have a purpose in the church. He's getting the younger generation so consumed with their careers, and raising families, and sporting events, and family events that they are too weary and too spent to get involved the way they need to. He's using our professions and our obsessions to rob us of our passion.

Now he's causing us to look at each other and blame the other for their problems. And there are no elders in the gates, and there are no young men playing music, and the city or the church is in a helpless state of indifference.

I am intrigued by the scene captured in 2 Samuel 21. The Bible says in verse 15 that Israel *"...was at war again..."* with the Philistines. And so, David went down with his servants and fought against the Philistines. But the Bible records a very unsettling statement... *"And David grew weary."*

> *"And Ishbi-benob, one of the descendants of the giants, whose spear weighed three hundred shekels of bronze, and who was armed with a new sword, thought to kill David."* (2 Samuel 21:16 ESV)

This is what the enemy wanted. A weary elder is vulnerable. I don't care how mighty a man of valor David was, David had been fighting for many years, and David had fought many great battles. He's an elder now, but he's weakened because he'd lost his purpose. David wasn't supposed to be out fighting giants anymore. He was supposed to train and equip a new, young, and mighty warriors to take his place. David no longer knew where he fit in in the kingdom of God, so David suited up for war and went out to fight the giant alone.

Here's the thing about David, David is the only giant killer in Israel. Is it because David was the only one anointed to kill a giant? No. It's because David missed an opportunity to develop the next generation of warriors.

> *"But Abishai the son of Zeruiah came to his aid and attacked the Philistine and killed him. Then David's men swore to him, 'You shall no longer go out with us to battle, lest you quench the lamp of Israel.'"* (2 Samuel 21:17 ESV)

Just when the giant thought he had David dead to rights, a young man named Abishai rushes in. The KJV says that Abishai succoured him, the ESV says, came to his aid. The word "succoured" means to stand in front of or protect. Instead of blaming David for his weakness, Abishai stood in front of David and said, *"if you want to get to him, you have to go through me."*

Abishai's name means "my father is a gift," and when the younger generation valued the older generation, God was pleased to anoint Abishai with the same abilities as David.

I want to encourage the older leaders who have been fighting for a while. You have stood in the trenches and have fought for generations. You might feel weary, and you might feel scared of where the church might be heading. However, take courage. There are still young people who value what you stood for. Young men and women are willing to stand beside you and defend you. I want to encourage you; the truth isn't dying with your generation. There are still some Abishai's out there who believe this thing just like you do.

The Solution

Let's look at what Peter said regarding the vision. He used the Greek word horasis "vision," which means –"to experience mentally or physically." In a world where leaders were mentally and physically exhausted, Peter saw a generation of followers who experienced this thing for themselves.

When Joel saw the church, he saw an elder/leader-dependent church. Yet when Peter saw the church, he didn't see a leader-dependent church. Peter saw a church that was follower-driven. Peter did not see a church that disregarded its leaders; instead, he saw a generation of followers who supported its leaders.

When Moses's followers, Aaron and Hur, took ownership of Israel's wellbeing, they didn't criticize Moses for being weary. Instead, they said, *"Moses, we're here to help you carry the load."*

II Kings 2 records a very unusual scene. She-bears devour a group of teenagers who were mocking the prophet, Elisha. Why did God kill them? The scripture says it was because they said, "Go up thou bald head."

We have no evidence that Elisha was bald, but we know that hair was connected to glory. You may remember a particular apostle covered this in I Corinthians 11 when he told the ladies that if they cut their hair, they may as well be shaven. Hair is representative of glory.

To be baldheaded was to be without glory, honor, or strength. Elisha had just taken the mantle of Elijah. He'd just assumed the role of elder, and these teenagers were essentially saying, *"You don't have glory, honor, or strength."*

God wasn't about to allow followers to question the integrity, the glory, or the honor of their man of God!

Had Aaron and Hur had that kind of spirit, Israel would've lost the battle that day. Instead, when their man of God got weary, Aaron and Hur didn't criticize. They didn't condemn. They said, pastor, let us help carry the load. Let us pray for the sick. Let us teach a Bible study. Let us visit the hospitals. Let us be involved!

The Bible tells us of Elisha: As he got older, he wasn't as strong as he'd once been. He began looking for a young man who could take his mantle and run with it.

> *"Now Elisha was fallen sick of his sickness whereof he died. And Joash the king of Israel came down unto him, and wept over his face, and said, 'O my father, my father, the chariot of Israel, and the horsemen thereof.'"* (II Kings 13:14-17)

Elisha symbolizes this generation of elders/leaders. Joash represents this generation of followers.

> *"And Elisha said unto him, 'Take bow and arrows.' And he took unto him bow and arrows. And he said to the king of Israel, 'Put thine hand upon the bow.' And he put his hand upon it: and Elisha put his hands upon the king's hands. And he said, 'Open the window eastward.' And he opened it. Then Elisha said, 'Shoot.' And he shot. And he said, 'The arrow of the Lord's deliverance, and the arrow of deliverance from Syria: for thou shalt smite the Syrians in Aphek, till thou have consumed them.'"*

As that young man picked up the bow in his hands and pointed that bow out the window, the old prophet stood behind him and placed his hands over the hands of Joash. The prophet said, *"Shoot,"* and the young man shot.

Notice it was the strength of a young man that shot the arrow of victory out of the window. But it was the guidance of old hands that guided the path of the arrow.

If the church is to remain a victorious church, we need young people's strength to drive this thing, and elders' guidance making sure we're going in the right direction.

followership

In the words of Daniel Bourdanné:

> "You can easily kill the dynamic of a student movement by being staff-led rather than student-led. If staff are doing it all, it is not helping students to grow... You are a gift to the next generation but also to your own generation. Choose today to learn leadership through following!"

The impact of a follower is more profound than the world lets us know. We spend all our time and energy praising organizations' leadership; however, if any organization is excellent, it results from great followers.

If we are to reach our potential, we need purpose-filled followers—followers who will pull back the arrow and allow leadership to provide the direction.

You can do it!

about the author
- joshua mcelhaney

Family EST. 2007

Joshua McElhaney has spent over 15 years in active ministry. During his years of service, Joshua has led from various leadership positions, including serving as an Assistant Pastor and serving as the Lead Pastor. In that time, Joshua trained leadership teams, built leadership systems, taught Theological College curriculum, and led his church through a rebrand and dynamic culture shift.

Joshua's passion also led him to start a graphic design company, PixelMonkey Designs, helping churches and small businesses establish their brand identity and marketing strategies. His love for writing and passion for helping other people realize their publication dreams led Joshua to launch Coffee House Publisher in 2019. Since then, Joshua has published or republished four of his books and has helped two authors publish their first projects. Joshua is looking to expand that business in the future and help many aspiring writers realize their dreams!

In June of 2007, Joshua married his college sweetheart Karena. Together they have three beautiful children. Mayli, Jaxson, and Asher. They love adventures, being outdoors, and especially their Friday night pizza and ice cream family nights!

You can follow Joshua on social media:

Facebook @joshuamcelhaney

Instagram @joshualmcelhaney

Twitter @jlmcelhaney

www.thecoffeehouseblog.com

www.pixelmonkey.design

Made in the USA
Monee, IL
19 May 2021